Domain-Driven Design Reference

Definitions and Pattern Summaries

Eric Evans

© 2015 Eric Evans
All Rights Reserved.

No part of this publication may be reproduced, stored in a retrieval system, or transmitted, in any form or by any means, electronic, mechanical, photocopying, recording, or otherwise, without the written permission of the author.

First published by Dog Ear Publishing
4010 W. 86th Street, Ste H
Indianapolis, IN 46268
www.dogearpublishing.net

ISBN: 978-145750-119-7

This book is printed on acid-free paper.

Printed in the United States of America

Contents

Acknowledgements vii

Definitions x

Pattern Language Overview xi

I: Putting the Model to Work 1
    Bounded Context 2
    Ubiquitous Language 4
    Continuous Integration 6
    Model-Driven Design 7
    Hands-on Modelers 8
    Refactoring Toward Deeper Insight 9

II: Building Blocks of a Model-Driven Design 10
    Layered Architecture 11
    Entities 13
    Value Objects 15
    Domain Events* 17
    Services 19
    Modules 20
    Aggregates 21
    Repositories 23
    Factories 25

III: Supple Design 26
- Intention-Revealing Interfaces 28
- Side-Effect-Free Functions 29
- Assertions 30
- Standalone Classes 31
- Closure of Operations.............................32
- Declarative Design 33
- A Declarative Style of Design.................33
- Drawing on Established Formalisms......35
- Conceptual Contours 36

IV: Context Mapping for Strategic Design 37
- Context Map..39
- Partnership* 41
- Shared Kernel 43
- Customer/Supplier Development...........45
- Conformist...46
- Anticorruption Layer 47
- Open-host Service 49
- Published Language................................50
- Separate Ways...51
- Big Ball of Mud* 53

V: Distillation for Strategic Design 55
Core Domain..56
Generic Subdomains......................................58
Domain Vision Statement.............................59
Highlighted Core...60
Cohesive Mechanisms 62
Segregated Core 63
Abstract Core..64

VI: Large-scale Structure for Strategic Design 66
Evolving Order 68
System Metaphor 69
Responsibility Layers 70
Knowledge Level...71
Pluggable Component Framework...............72
Photo Credits..73
Other Credits 74

* New term introduced since the 2004 book.

Acknowledgements

It has now been over ten year since the publication of my book, *Domain-Driven Design, Tackling Complexity in the Heart of Software (*or "The Big Blue Book", as some people have taken to calling it). In that decade, the fundamentals discussed in the book haven't changed much, but a *lot* has changed about how we build software. DDD has stayed relevant because smart and innovative people have shaken things up repeatedly. I want to thank those people.

Let me start with Greg Young, Udi Dahan and the people inspired by them, for CQRS and Event Sourcing. These are now quite mainstream options for the architecture of a DDD system. This was the first successful big departure from the narrow view of architecture inherited from the turn of the century.

Since then, there have been several interesting technologies and frameworks that had a goal of making DDD more concrete in implementation (among other goals of their designers), with varying degrees of success. These include Qi4J, Naked Objects, Roo, and others. Such experiments have great value, even when they don't gain wide adoption.

I also want to thank the people and communities that have revolutionized our technical ecosystem in recent years in ways that make DDD much more fun and practical. Most of these people have minimal interest in DDD, but their work has benefited us tremendously. I'm particularly thinking of the freedom NoSQL is bringing us, the reduced syntactical-noise of new programming languages (some functional), and the relentless drive toward lighter technical frameworks and unintrusive, decoupled libraries. The technology of a decade ago was complicated and heavy, and made DDD even more difficult. There is bad new technology too, of course, but the trend is good. So I extend a special thanks to all those who have contributed to this trend, though you may never have heard of DDD.

Next, I want to thank those who have written books about DDD. The first book about DDD after mine was by Jimmy Nilsson. With one book, you have a book. With two, you have a topic. Next, InfoQ published *DDD Quickly*, which, because of its brevity, its availability as a free download and the reach of InfoQ, gave a lot of people their first taste of the topic. The years went by, and there were many valuable blog articles and other short-form writings. There were also specialty books such as *DDD with Naked Objects*. And I particularly want to thank the indispensable Martin Fowler, who has helped to clearly communicate the concepts of DDD as well as often providing the definitive documentation of emerging patterns. Just last year, Vaughn Vernon published the most ambitious book since my own, *Implementing Domain-Driven Design* (which some seem to be calling "The Big Red Book").

I feel a kind of despair over the inevitability that I will leave out many people who made significant contributions, and I am genuinely sorry about that. Let me at least give a blanket thank you to the people who have pushed DDD out into the public view and to those who have pushed DDD into quiet corners of organizations. It takes thousands of champions for a software philosophy to have any impact.

Although this is the first print edition of the DDD reference, the earliest form actually predates the publication of my 2004 book. On the advice of Ralph Johnson, I extracted the brief summaries of each pattern and used them in workshops, with each pattern being read aloud by attendees followed by discussion. I used those documents in training classes for several years.

Then, a few years after my book was published, Ward Cunningham, as part of his work on a patterns repository, proposed to a few authors that we put short summaries of our patterns into the Creative Commons. Martin Fowler and I, with the agreement of Pearson Education, our publisher, did just that, which opened up possibilities for derivative works, such as this one.

Thank you all.

Eric Evans, June 2014

Definitions

domain

A sphere of knowledge, influence, or activity. The subject area to which the user applies a program is the domain of the software.

model

A system of abstractions that describes selected aspects of a domain and can be used to solve problems related to that domain.

ubiquitous language

A language structured around the domain model and used by all team members within a bounded context to connect all the activities of the team with the software.

context

The setting in which a word or statement appears that determines its meaning. *Statements about a model can only be understood in a context.*

bounded context (see pattern)

A description of a boundary (typically a subsystem, or the work of a particular team) within which a particular model is defined and applicable.

Pattern Language Overview

I:
Putting the Model to Work

Domain-Driven Design is an approach to the development of complex software in which we:

1. Focus on the *core domain*.
2. Explore *models* in a creative collaboration of domain practitioners and software practitioners.
3. Speak a *ubiquitous language* within an explicitly *bounded context*.

This three-point summary of DDD depends on the definition of the terms, which are defined in this booklet.

Many projects do modeling work without getting much real benefit in the end. The patterns of DDD distill successful practices from projects where dramatic benefits have come from modeling. Taken together, they lay out a quite different approach to modeling and software development that runs from fine details to high-level vision. Rigorous modeling conventions must be balanced with free exploration of models in collaboration with non-technical people. Tactics and strategy must be combined to succeed, and DDD addresses both tactical and strategic design.

Bounded Context

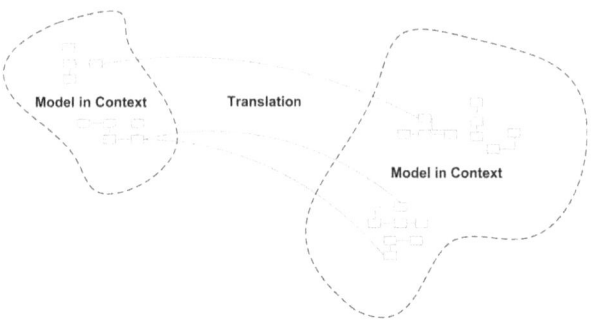

Multiple models are in play on any large project. They emerge for many reasons. Two subsystems commonly serve very different user communities, with different jobs, where different models may be useful. Teams working independently may solve the same problem in different ways through lack of communication. The tool set may also be different, meaning that program code cannot be shared.

Multiple models are inevitable, yet when code based on distinct models is combined, software becomes buggy, unreliable, and difficult to understand. Communication among team members becomes confused. It is often unclear in what context a model should not be applied.

Model expressions, like any other phrase, only have meaning in context.

Therefore:
Explicitly define the context within which a model applies. Explicitly set boundaries in terms of team organization, usage within specific parts of the application, and physical manifestations such as code bases and database schemas. Apply Continuous Integration to keep model concepts and

terms strictly consistent within these bounds, but don't be distracted or confused by issues outside. Standardize a single development process within the context, which need not be used elsewhere.

Ubiquitous Language

> For first you write a sentence,
> And then you chop it small;
> Then mix the bits, and sort them out
> Just as they chance to fall:
> The order of the phrases makes
> No difference at all.
>
> —Lewis Carroll, "Poeta Fit, Non Nascitur"

To create a supple, knowledge-rich design calls for a versatile, shared team language, and a lively experimentation with language that seldom happens on software projects.

Within a single *bounded context*, language can be fractured in ways that undermine efforts to apply sophisticated modeling. If the model is only used to draw UML diagrams for the technical members of the team, then it is not contributing to the creative collaboration at the heart of DDD.

Domain experts use their jargon while technical team members have their own language tuned for discussing the domain in terms of design. The terminology of day-to-day discussions is disconnected from the terminology embedded in the code (ultimately the most important product of a software project). And even the same person uses different language in speech and in writing, so that the most incisive expressions of the domain often emerge in a transient form that is never captured in the code or even in writing.

Translation blunts communication and makes knowledge crunching anemic.

Yet none of these dialects can be a common language because none serves all needs.

Domain experts should object to terms or structures that are awkward or inadequate to convey domain understanding; developers should watch for ambiguity or inconsistency that will trip up design.

Play with the model as you talk about the system. Describe scenarios *out loud* using the elements and interactions of the model, combining concepts in ways allowed by the model. Find easier ways to say what you need to say, and then take those new ideas back down to the diagrams and code.

With a *ubiquitous language*, the model is not just a design artifact. It becomes integral to everything the developers and domain experts do together.

Therefore:
Use the model as the backbone of a language. Commit the team to exercising that language relentlessly in all communication within the team and in the code. Within a bounded context, use the same language in diagrams, writing, and especially speech.

Recognize that a change in the language is a change to the model.

Iron out difficulties by experimenting with alternative expressions, which reflect alternative models. Then refactor the code, renaming classes, methods, and modules to conform to the new model. Resolve confusion over terms in conversation, in just the way we come to agree on the meaning of ordinary words.

Continuous Integration
Once a bounded context has been defined, we must keep it sound.

Photo: Christopher Schmidt

When a number of people are working in the same bounded context, there is a strong tendency for the model to fragment. The bigger the team, the bigger the problem, but as few as three or four people can encounter serious problems. Yet breaking down the system into ever-smaller contexts eventually loses a valuable level of integration and coherency.

Therefore:
Institute a process of merging all code and other implementation artifacts frequently, with automated tests to flag fragmentation quickly. Relentlessly exercise the ubiquitous language to hammer out a shared view of the model as the concepts evolve in different people's heads.

Model-Driven Design

Tightly relating the code to an underlying model gives the code meaning and makes the model relevant.

If the design, or some central part of it, does not map to the domain model, that model is of little value, and the correctness of the software is suspect. At the same time, complex mappings between models and design functions are difficult to understand and, in practice, impossible to maintain as the design changes. A deadly divide opens between analysis and design so that insight gained in each of those activities does not feed into the other.

Draw from the model the terminology used in the design and the basic assignment of responsibilities. The code becomes an expression of the model, so a change to the code may be a change to the model. Its effect must ripple through the rest of the project's activities accordingly.

To tie the implementation slavishly to a model usually requires software development tools and languages that support a modeling paradigm, such as object-oriented programming.

Therefore:

Design a portion of the software system to reflect the domain model in a very literal way, so that mapping is obvious. Revisit the model and modify it to be implemented more naturally in software, even as you seek to make it reflect deeper insight into the domain. Demand a single model that serves both purposes well, in addition to supporting a fluent ubiquitous language.

Hands-on Modelers

If the people who write the code do not feel responsible for the model, or don't understand how to make the model work for an application, then the model has nothing to do with the software. If developers don't realize that changing code changes the model, then their refactoring will weaken the model rather than strengthen it. Meanwhile, when a modeler is separated from the implementation process, he or she never acquires, or quickly loses, a feel for the constraints of implementation. The basic constraint of model-driven design—that the model supports an effective implementation and abstracts key insights into the domain—is half-gone, and the resulting models will be impractical. Finally, the knowledge and skills of experienced designers won't be transferred to other developers if the division of labor prevents the kind of collaboration that conveys the subtleties of coding a model-driven design.

Therefore:
Any technical person contributing to the model must spend some time touching the code, whatever primary role he or she plays on the project. Anyone responsible for changing code must learn to express a model through the code. Every developer must be involved in some level of discussion about the model and have contact with domain experts. Those who contribute in different ways must consciously engage those who touch the code in a dynamic exchange of model ideas through the ubiquitous language.

Refactoring Toward Deeper Insight

Using a proven set of basic building blocks along with consistent language brings some sanity to the development effort. This leaves the challenge of actually finding an incisive model, one that captures subtle concerns of the domain experts and can drive a practical design. A model that sloughs off the superficial and captures the essential is a deep model. This should make the software more in tune with the way the domain experts think and more responsive to the user's needs.

Traditionally, refactoring is described in terms of code transformations with technical motivations. Refactoring can also be motivated by an insight into the domain and a corresponding refinement of the model or its expression in code.

Sophisticated domain models seldom turn out useful except when developed through an iterative process of refactoring, including close involvement of the domain experts with developers interested in learning about the domain.

II:
Building Blocks of a Model-Driven Design

These patterns cast widely held best practices of object-oriented design in the light of domain-driven design. They guide decisions to clarify the model and to keep the model and implementation aligned with each other, each reinforcing the other's effectiveness. Careful crafting the details of individual model elements gives developers a steady platform from which to explore models and to keep them in close correspondence with the implementation.

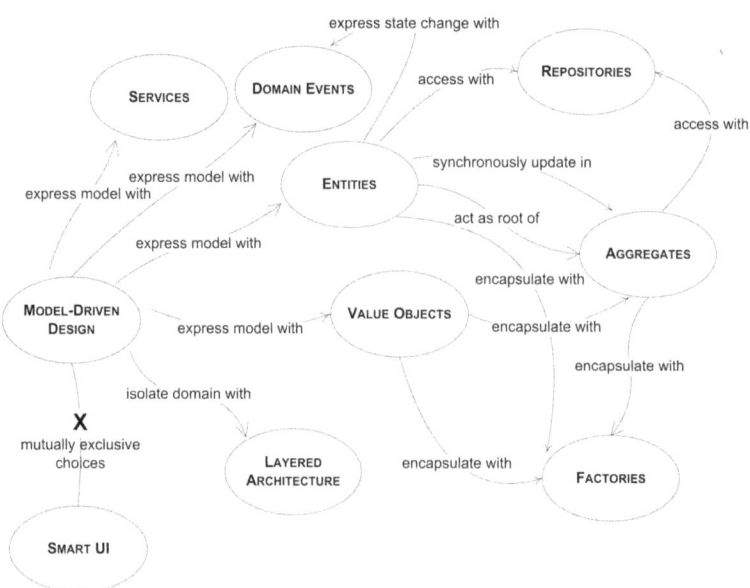

Layered Architecture

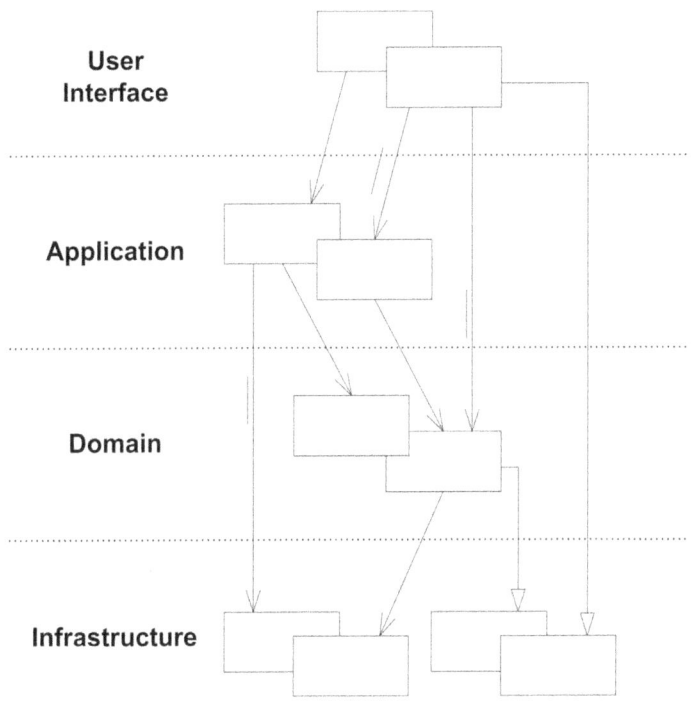

In an object-oriented program, UI, database, and other support code often gets written directly into the business objects. Additional business logic is embedded in the behavior of UI widgets and database scripts. This happens because it is the easiest way to make things work, in the short run.

When the domain-related code is diffused through such a large amount of other code, it becomes extremely difficult to see and to reason about. Superficial changes to the UI can actually change business logic. To change a business rule may require meticulous tracing of UI code, database code, or other program elements. Implementing coherent, model-driven objects becomes impractical. Automated testing is awkward. With all the technologies and logic involved in each activity, a program must be kept very simple or it becomes impossible to understand.

Therefore:
Isolate the expression of the domain model and the business logic, and eliminate any dependency on infrastructure, user interface, or even application logic that is not business logic. Partition a complex program into layers. Develop a design within each layer that is cohesive and that depends only on the layers below. Follow standard architectural patterns to provide loose coupling to the layers above. Concentrate all the code related to the domain model in one layer and isolate it from the user interface, application, and infrastructure code. The domain objects, free of the responsibility of displaying themselves, storing themselves, managing application tasks, and so forth, can be focused on expressing the domain model. This allows a model to evolve to be rich enough and clear enough to capture essential business knowledge and put it to work.

The key goal here is isolation. Related patterns, such as "Hexagonal Architecture" may serve as well or better to the degree that they allow our domain model expressions to avoid dependencies on and references to other system concerns.

Entities

Many objects represent a thread of continuity and identity, going through a lifecycle, though their attributes may change.

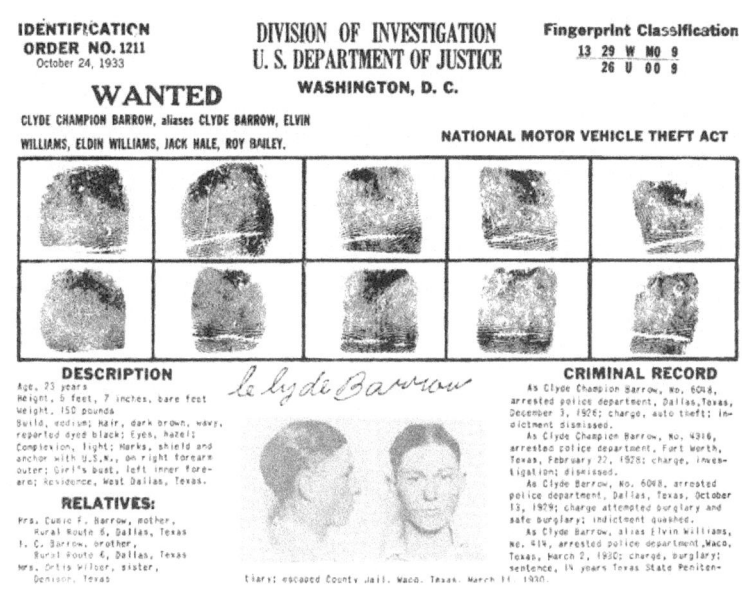

Wanted Poster for Clyde Barrow (of Bonnie & Clyde)

Some objects are not defined primarily by their attributes. They represent a thread of identity that runs through time and often across distinct representations. Sometimes such an object must be matched with another object even though attributes differ. An object must be distinguished from other objects even though they might have the same attributes. Mistaken identity can lead to data corruption.

Therefore:

When an object is distinguished by its identity, rather than its attributes, make this primary to its definition in the model. Keep the class definition simple and focused on life cycle continuity and identity.

Define a means of distinguishing each object regardless of its form or history. Be alert to requirements that call for matching objects by attributes. Define an operation that is guaranteed to produce a unique result for each object, possibly by attaching a symbol that is guaranteed unique. This means of identification may come from the outside, or it may be an arbitrary identifier created by and for the system, but it must correspond to the identity distinctions in the model.

The model must define what it means to be the same thing.

(aka Reference Objects)

Value Objects

Some objects describe or compute some characteristic of a thing.

Many objects have no conceptual identity.

Tracking the identity of entities is essential, but attaching identity to other objects can hurt system performance, add analytical work, and muddle the model by making all objects look the same. Software design is a constant battle with complexity. We must make distinctions so that special handling is applied only where necessary.

However, if we think of this category of object as just the absence of identity, we haven't added much to our toolbox or vocabulary. In fact, these objects have characteristics of their own, and their own significance to the model. These are the objects that describe things.

Therefore:

When you care only about the attributes and logic of an element of the model, classify it as a value object. Make it express the meaning of the attributes it conveys and give it related functionality. Treat the value object as immutable. Make all operations Side-effect-free Functions that don't depend on any mutable state. Don't give a value object any identity and avoid the design complexities necessary to maintain entities.

Domain Events

Something happened that domain experts care about.

Safe or out?

An *entity* is responsible for tracking its state and the rules regulating its lifecycle. But if you need to know the actual causes of the state changes, this is typically not explicit, and it may be difficult to explain how the system got the way it is. Audit trails can allow tracing, but are not usually suited to being used for the logic of the program itself. Change histories of entities can allow access to previous states, but ignores the meaning of those changes, so that any manipulation of the information is procedural, and often pushed out of the domain layer.

A distinct, though related set of issues arises in distributed systems. The state of a distributed system cannot be kept completely consistent at all times. We keep the aggregates internally consistent at all times, while making other changes asynchronously. As changes propagate across nodes of a network, it can be difficult to resolve multiple updates arriving out of order or from distinct sources.

Therefore:
Model information about activity in the domain as a series of discrete events. Represent each event as a domain object. These are distinct from system events that reflect activity within the software itself, although often a system event is associated with a domain event, either as part of a response to the domain event or as a way of carrying information about the domain event into the system.

A domain event is a full-fledged part of the domain model, a representation of something that happened in the domain. Ignore irrelevant domain activity while making explicit the events that the domain experts want to track or be notified of, or which are associated with state change in the other model objects.

In a distributed system, the state of an entity can be inferred from the domain events currently known to a particular node, allowing a coherent model in the absence of full information about the system as a whole.

Domain events are ordinarily immutable, as they are a record of something in the past. In addition to a description of the event, a domain event typically contains a timestamp for the time the event occurred and the identity of entities involved in the event. Also, a domain event often has a separate timestamp indicating when the event was entered into the system and the identity of the person who entered it. When useful, an identity for the domain event can be based on some set of these properties. So, for example, if two instances of the same event arrive at a node they can be recognized as the same.

Services

Sometimes, it just isn't a thing.

Some concepts from the domain aren't natural to model as objects. Forcing the required domain functionality to be the responsibility of an entity or value either distorts the definition of a model-based object or adds meaningless artificial objects.

Therefore:
When a significant process or transformation in the domain is not a natural responsibility of an entity or value object, add an operation to the model as a standalone interface declared as a service. Define a service contract, a set of assertions about interactions with the service. (See assertions.) State these assertions in the ubiquitous language of a specific bounded context. Give the service a name, which also becomes part of the ubiquitous language.

Modules

Everyone uses modules, but few treat them as a full-fledged part of the model. Code gets broken down into all sorts of categories, from aspects of the technical architecture to developers' work assignments. Even developers who refactor a lot tend to content themselves with modules conceived early in the project.

Explanations of coupling and cohesion tend to make them sound like technical metrics, to be judged mechanically based on the distributions of associations and interactions. Yet *it isn't just code being divided into modules, but also concepts*. There is a limit to how many things a person can think about at once (hence low coupling). Incoherent fragments of ideas are as hard to understand as an undifferentiated soup of ideas (hence high cohesion).

Therefore:
Choose modules that tell the story of the system and contain a cohesive set of concepts. Give the modules names that become part of the ubiquitous language. Modules are part of the model and their names should reflect insight into the domain.

This often yields low coupling between modules, but if it doesn't look for a way to change the model to disentangle the concepts, or an overlooked concept that might be the basis of a module that would bring the elements together in a meaningful way. Seek low coupling in the sense of concepts that can be understood and reasoned about independently. Refine the model until it partitions according to high-level domain concepts and the corresponding code is decoupled as well.

(aka Packages)

Aggregates

Photo: Martine Jousset

It is difficult to guarantee the consistency of changes to objects in a model with complex associations. Objects are supposed to maintain their own internal consistent state, but they can be blindsided by changes in other objects that are conceptually constituent parts. Cautious database locking schemes cause multiple users to interfere pointlessly with each other and can make a system unusable. Similar issues arise when distributing objects among multiple servers, or designing asynchronous transactions.

Therefore:
Cluster the entities and value objects into aggregates and define boundaries around each. Choose one entity to be the root of each aggregate, and allow external objects to hold references to the root only (references to internal members passed out for use within a single operation only). Define properties and invariants for the aggregate as

a whole and give enforcement responsibility to the root or some designated framework mechanism.

Use the same aggregate boundaries to govern transactions and distribution.

Within an aggregate boundary, apply consistency rules synchronously. Across boundaries, handle updates asynchronously.

Keep an aggregate together on one server. Allow different aggregates to be distributed among nodes.

When these design decisions are not being guided well by the aggregate boundaries, reconsider the model. Is the domain scenario hinting at an important new insight? Such changes often improve the model's expressiveness and flexibility as well as resolving the transactional and distributional issues.

Repositories

Query access to aggregates expressed in the ubiquitous language.

Proliferation of traversable associations used only for finding things muddles the model. In mature models, queries often express domain concepts. Yet queries can cause problems.

The sheer technical complexity of applying most database access infrastructure quickly swamps the client code, which leads developers to dumb-down the domain layer, which makes the model irrelevant.

A query framework may encapsulate most of that technical complexity, enabling developers to pull the exact data they need from the database in a more automated or declarative way, but that only solves part of the problem.

Unconstrained queries may pull specific fields from objects, breaching encapsulation, or instantiate a few specific objects from the interior of an aggregate, blindsiding the aggregate root and making it impossible for these objects to enforce the rules of the domain model. Domain logic moves into queries and application layer code, and the entities and value objects become mere data containers.

Therefore:
For each type of aggregate that needs global access, create a service that can provide the illusion of an in-memory collection of all objects of that aggregate's root type. Set up access through a well-known global interface. Provide methods to add and remove objects, which will encapsulate the actual insertion or removal of data in the data store. Provide methods that select objects based on criteria meaningful to domain experts. Return fully instantiated

objects or collections of objects whose attribute values meet the criteria, thereby encapsulating the actual storage and query technology, or return proxies that give the illusion of fully instantiated aggregates in a lazy way. Provide repositories only for aggregate roots that actually need direct access. Keep application logic focused on the model, delegating all object storage and access to the repositories.

Factories

When creation of an entire, internally consistent aggregate, or a large value object, becomes complicated or reveals too much of the internal structure, factories provide encapsulation.

Creation of an object can be a major operation in itself, but complex assembly operations do not fit the responsibility of the created objects. Combining such responsibilities can produce ungainly designs that are hard to understand. Making the client direct construction muddies the design of the client, breaches encapsulation of the assembled object or aggregate, and overly couples the client to the implementation of the created object.

Therefore:

Shift the responsibility for creating instances of complex objects and aggregates to a separate object, which may itself have no responsibility in the domain model but is still part of the domain design. Provide an interface that encapsulates all complex assembly and that does not require the client to reference the concrete classes of the objects being instantiated. Create an entire aggregate as a piece, enforcing its invariants. Create a complex value object as a piece, possibly after assembling the elements with a builder.

III
Supple Design

To have a project accelerate as development proceeds—rather than get weighed down by its own legacy—demands a design that is a pleasure to work with, inviting to change. A *supple design*.

Supple design is the complement to deep modeling.

Developers play two roles, each of which must be served by the design. The same person might well play both roles—even switch back and forth in minutes—but the relationship to the code is different nonetheless. One role is the developer of a client, who weaves the domain objects into the application code or other domain layer code, utilizing capabilities of the design. A supple design reveals a deep underlying model that makes its potential clear. The client developer can flexibly use a minimal set of loosely coupled concepts to express a range of scenarios in the domain. Design elements fit together in a natural way with a result that is predictable, clearly characterized, and robust.

Equally important, the design must serve the developer working to change it. To be open to change, a design must be easy to understand, revealing that same underlying model that the client developer is drawing on. It must follow the contours of a deep model of the domain, so most changes bend the design at flexible points. The effects of its code must be transparently obvious, so the consequences of a change will be easy to anticipate.

- Making behavior obvious
- Reducing the cost of change
- Creating software developers to work with

Intention-Revealing Interfaces

If a developer must consider the implementation of a component in order to use it, the value of encapsulation is lost. If someone other than the original developer must infer the purpose of an object or operation based on its implementation, that new developer may infer a purpose that the operation or class fulfills only by chance. If that was not the intent, the code may work for the moment, but the conceptual basis of the design will have been corrupted, and the two developers will be working at cross-purposes.

Therefore:
Name classes and operations to describe their effect and purpose, without reference to the means by which they do what they promise. This relieves the client developer of the need to understand the internals. These names should conform to the ubiquitous language so that team members can quickly infer their meaning. Write a test for a behavior before creating it, to force your thinking into client developer mode.

Side-Effect-Free Functions

Interactions of multiple rules or compositions of calculations become extremely difficult to predict. The developer calling an operation must understand its implementation and the implementation of all its delegations in order to anticipate the result. The usefulness of any abstraction of interfaces is limited if the developers are forced to pierce the veil. Without safely predictable abstractions, the developers must limit the combinatory explosion, placing a low ceiling on the richness of behavior that is feasible to build.

Therefore:
Place as much of the logic of the program as possible into functions, operations that return results with no observable side effects. Strictly segregate commands (methods which result in modifications to observable state) into very simple operations that do not return domain information. Further control side effects by moving complex logic into value objects when a concept fitting the responsibility presents itself.

All operations of a value object should be side-effect-free functions.

Assertions

When the side effects of operations are only defined implicitly by their implementation, designs with a lot of delegation become a tangle of cause and effect. The only way to understand a program is to trace execution through branching paths. The value of encapsulation is lost. The necessity of tracing concrete execution defeats abstraction.

Therefore:

State post-conditions of operations and invariants of classes and aggregates. If assertions cannot be coded directly in your programming language, write automated unit tests for them. Write them into documentation or diagrams where it fits the style of the project's development process.

Seek models with coherent sets of concepts, which lead a developer to infer the intended assertions, accelerating the learning curve and reducing the risk of contradictory code.

Assertions define contracts of services and entity modifiers.

Assertions define invariants on aggregates.

Standalone Classes

Even within a module, the difficulty of interpreting a design increases wildly as dependencies are added. This adds to mental overload, limiting the design complexity a developer can handle. Implicit concepts contribute to this load even more than explicit references.

Low coupling is fundamental to object design. When you can, go all the way. Eliminate all other concepts from the picture. Then the class will be completely self-contained and can be studied and understood alone. Every such self-contained class significantly eases the burden of understanding a module.

Closure of Operations

Most interesting objects end up doing things that can't be characterized by primitives alone.

Therefore:
Where it fits, define an operation whose return type is the same as the type of its argument(s). If the implementer has state that is used in the computation, then the implementer is effectively an argument of the operation, so the argument(s) and return value should be of the same type as the implementer. Such an operation is closed under the set of instances of that type. A closed operation provides a high-level interface without introducing any dependency on other concepts.

This pattern is most often applied to the operations of a value object. Because the life cycle of an entity has significance in the domain, you can't just conjure up a new one to answer a question. There are operations that are closed under an entity type. You could ask an Employee object for its supervisor and get back another Employee. But in general, entities are not the sort of concepts that are likely to be the result of a computation. So, for the most part, this is an opportunity to look for in the value objects.

You sometimes get halfway to this pattern. The argument matches the implementer, but the return type is different, or the return type matches the receiver and the argument is different. These operations are not closed, but they do give some of the advantage of closure, in freeing the mind.

Declarative Design

There can be no real guarantees in procedural software. To name just one way of evading assertions, code could have additional side effects that were not specifically excluded. No matter how model-driven our design is, we still end up writing procedures to produce the effect of the conceptual interactions. And we spend much of our time writing boilerplate code that doesn't really add any meaning or behavior. Intention-revealing interfaces and the other patterns in this chapter help, but they can never give conventional object-oriented programs formal rigor.

These are some of the motivations behind declarative design. This term means many things to many people, but usually it indicates a way to write a program, or some part of a program, as a kind of executable specification. A very precise description of properties actually controls the software. In its various forms, this could be done through a reflection mechanism or at compile time through code generation (producing conventional code automatically, based on the declaration). This approach allows another developer to take the declaration at face value. It is an absolute guarantee.

Many declarative approaches can be corrupted if the developers bypass them intentionally or unintentionally. This is likely when the system is difficult to use or overly restrictive. Everyone has to follow the rules of the framework in order to get the benefits of a declarative program.

A Declarative Style of Design

Once your design has intention-revealing interfaces, side-effect-free functions, and assertions, you are edging into declarative territory. Many of the benefits of declarative design are obtained once you have combinable elements that communicate their meaning, and have characterized or obvious effects, or no observable effects at all.

A supple design can make it possible for the client code to use a declarative style of design. To illustrate, the next section will bring together some of the patterns in this chapter to make the specification more supple and declarative.

Drawing on Established Formalisms

Creating a tight conceptual framework from scratch is something you can't do every day. Sometimes you discover and refine one of these over the course of the life of a project. But you can often use and adapt conceptual systems that are long established in your domain or others, some of which have been refined and distilled over centuries. Many business applications involve accounting, for example. Accounting defines a well-developed set of entities and rules that make for an easy adaptation to a deep model and a supple design.

There are many such formalized conceptual frameworks, but my personal favorite is math. It is surprising how useful it can be to pull out some twist on basic arithmetic. Many domains include math somewhere. Look for it. Dig it out. Specialized math is clean, combinable by clear rules, and people find it easy to understand.

A real-world example, "Shares Math," was discussed in Chapter 8 of the book, Domain-Driven Design.

Conceptual Contours

Sometimes people chop functionality fine to allow flexible combination. Sometimes they lump it large to encapsulate complexity. Sometimes they seek a consistent granularity, making all classes and operations to a similar scale. These are oversimplifications that don't work well as general rules. But they are motivated by basic problems.

When elements of a model or design are embedded in a monolithic construct, their functionality gets duplicated. The external interface doesn't say everything a client might care about. Their meaning is hard to understand, because different concepts are mixed together.

Conversely, breaking down classes and methods can pointlessly complicate the client, forcing client objects to understand how tiny pieces fit together. Worse, a concept can be lost completely. Half of a uranium atom is not uranium. And of course, it isn't just grain size that counts, but just where the grain runs.

Therefore:
Decompose design elements (operations, interfaces, classes, and aggregates) into cohesive units, taking into consideration your intuition of the important divisions in the domain. Observe the axes of change and stability through successive refactorings and look for the underlying conceptual contours that explain these shearing patterns. Align the model with the consistent aspects of the domain that make it a viable area of knowledge in the first place.

A supple design based on a deep model yields a simple set of interfaces that combine logically to make sensible statements in the ubiquitous language, and without the distraction and maintenance burden of irrelevant options.

IV
Context Mapping for Strategic Design

bounded context (see pattern)

A description of a boundary (typically a subsystem, or the work of a particular team) within which a particular model is defined and applicable.

upstream-downstream

A relationship between two groups in which the "upstream" group's actions affect project success of the "downstream" group, but the actions of the downstream do not significantly affect projects upstream. (e.g. If two cities are along the same river, the upstream city's pollution primarily affects the downstream city.)

The upstream team may succeed independently of the fate of the downstream team.

mutually dependent

A situation in which two software development projects in separate contexts must both be delivered in order for either to be considered a success. (When two systems each rely on information or functionality of the other - something we would generally try to avoid - naturally we see the projects that build them as interdependent. Yet there are also mutually dependent projects where system dependencies run only one direction. When the depended-on system has little value without the dependent system and the integration with that system -perhaps because this is the only place it is used - then a failure to deliver the dependent system would be a failure of both projects.)

free

A software development context in which the direction, success or failure of development work in other contexts has little affect on delivery.

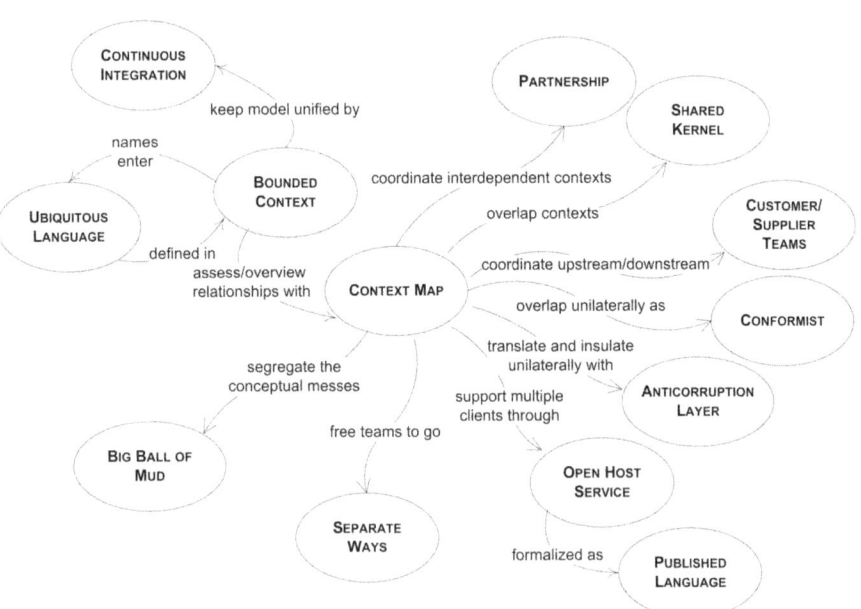

Context Map

To plot strategy, we need a realistic, large-scale view of model development extending across our project and others we integrate with.

An individual bounded context leaves some problems in the absence of a global view. The context of other models may still be vague and in flux.

People on other teams won't be very aware of the context boundaries and will unknowingly make changes that blur the edges or complicate the interconnections. When connections must be made between different contexts, they tend to bleed into each other.

Even when boundaries are clear, relationships with other contexts place constraints on the nature of model or pace of change that is feasible. These constraints manifest themselves primarily through non-technical channels that are sometimes hard to relate to the design decisions they are affecting.

Therefore:
Identify each model in play on the project and define its bounded context. This includes the implicit models of non-object-oriented subsystems. Name each bounded context, and make the names part of the ubiquitous language.

Describe the points of contact between the models, outlining explicit translation for any communication, highlighting any sharing, isolation mechanisms, and levels of influence.

Map the existing terrain. Take up transformations later.

This map can be a basis for realistic design strategy.

The characterization of relationships is made more concrete in the following pages, with a set of common patterns of relationships between bounded contexts.

Partnership

When teams in two contexts will succeed or fail together, a cooperative relationship often emerges.

Poor coordination of mutually dependent subsystems in separate contexts leads to delivery failure for both projects. A key feature missing from one system might make the other system undeliverable. Interfaces that do not match the expectations of the developers of the other subsystem could cause integration to fail. A mutually agreed interface might turn out to be so awkward to use that it slows the development of the client system, or so difficult to implement that it slows the development of the server subsystem. Failure brings both projects down.

Therefore:
Where development failure in either of two contexts would result in delivery failure for both, forge a partnership between the teams in charge of the two contexts. Institute a process for coordinated planning of development and joint management of integration.

The teams must cooperate on the evolution of their interfaces to accommodate the development needs of both

systems. Interdependent features should be scheduled so that they are completed for the same release.

It is not necessary, most of the time, for developers to understand the model of the other subsystem in detail, but they must coordinate their project planning. When development in one context hits obstacles, then joint examination of the issue is called for, to find an expeditious design solution that does not overly compromise either context.

Also, a clear process is needed to govern integration. For example, a special test suite can be defined that proves the interface meets the expectations of the client system, which can be run as part of continuous integration on the server system.

Shared Kernel

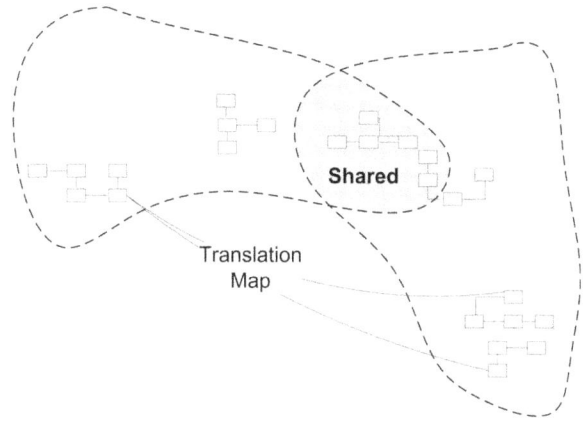

Sharing a part of the model and associated code is a very intimate interdependency, which can leverage design work or undermine it.

When functional integration is limited, the overhead of continuous integration of a large context may be deemed too high. This may especially be true when the team does not have the skill or the political organization to maintain continuous integration, or when a single team is simply too big and unwieldy. So separate bounded contexts might be defined and multiple teams formed.

Once separate, uncoordinated teams working on closely related applications can go racing forward for a while, but what they produce may not fit together. Even partner teams can end up spending a great deal on translation layers and retrofitting, meanwhile duplicating effort and losing the benefits of a common ubiquitous language.

Therefore:

Designate with an explicit boundary some subset of the domain model that the teams agree to share. Keep this kernel small.

Within this boundary, include, along with this subset of the model, the subset of code or of the database design associated with that part of the model. This explicitly shared stuff has special status, and shouldn't be changed without consultation with the other team.

Define a continuous integration process that will keep the kernel model tight and align the ubiquitous language of the teams. Integrate a functional system frequently, though somewhat less often than the pace of continuous integration within the teams.

Customer/Supplier Development

When two teams are in an upstream-downstream relationship, where the upstream team may succeed independently of the fate of the downstream team, the needs of the downstream come to be addressed in a variety of ways with a wide range of consequences.

A downstream team can be helpless, at the mercy of upstream priorities. Meanwhile, the upstream team may be inhibited, worried about breaking downstream systems. The problems of the downstream team are not improved by cumbersome change request procedures with complex approval processes. And the freewheeling development of the upstream team will stop if the downstream team has veto power over changes.

Therefore:
Establish a clear customer/supplier relationship between the two teams, meaning downstream priorities factor into upstream planning. Negotiate and budget tasks for downstream requirements so that everyone understands the commitment and schedule.

Agile teams can make the downstream team play the customer role to the upstream team, in planning sessions. Jointly developed automated acceptance tests can validate the expected interface from the upstream. Adding these tests to the upstream team's test suite, to be run as part of its continuous integration, will free the upstream team to make changes without fear of side effects downstream.

Conformist

When two development teams have an upstream/downstream relationship in which the upstream has no motivation to provide for the downstream team's needs, the downstream team is helpless. Altruism may motivate upstream developers to make promises, but they are unlikely to be fulfilled. Belief in those good intentions leads the downstream team to make plans based on features that will never be available. The downstream project will be delayed until the team ultimately learns to live with what it is given. An interface tailored to the needs of the downstream team is not in the cards.

Therefore:
Eliminate the complexity of translation between bounded contexts by slavishly adhering to the model of the upstream team. Although this cramps the style of the downstream designers and probably does not yield the ideal model for the application, choosing conformity enormously simplifies integration. Also, you will share a ubiquitous language with your upstream team. The upstream is in the driver's seat, so it is good to make communication easy for them. Altruism may be sufficient to get them to share information with you.

Anticorruption Layer

Translation layers can be simple, even elegant, when bridging well-designed bounded contexts with cooperative teams. But when control or communication is not adequate to pull off a shared kernel, partner or customer/supplier relationship, translation becomes more complex. The translation layer takes on a more defensive tone.

Photo: US National Oceanic and Atmospheric Administration

A large interface with an upstream system can eventually overwhelm the intent of the downstream model altogether, causing it to be modified to resemble the other system's model in an ad hoc fashion. The models of legacy systems are usually weak (if not *big balls of mud*), and even the exception that is clearly designed may not fit the needs of the current project, making it impractical to conform to the upstream model. Yet the integration may be very valuable or even required for the downstream project.

Therefore:
As a downstream client, create an isolating layer to provide your system with functionality of the upstream system in

terms of your own domain model. This layer talks to the other system through its existing interface, requiring little or no modification to the other system. Internally, the layer translates in one or both directions as necessary between the two models.

Open-host Service

Typically for each bounded context, you will define a translation layer for each component with which you have to integrate that is outside the context. Where integration is one-off, this approach of inserting a translation layer for each external system avoids corruption of the models with a minimum of cost. But when you find your subsystem in high demand, you may need a more flexible approach.

When a subsystem has to be integrated with many others, customizing a translator for each can bog down the team. There is more and more to maintain, and more and more to worry about when changes are made.

Therefore:
Define a protocol that gives access to your subsystem as a set of services. Open the protocol so that all who need to integrate with you can use it. Enhance and expand the protocol to handle new integration requirements, except when a single team has idiosyncratic needs. Then, use a one-off translator to augment the protocol for that special case so that the shared protocol can stay simple and coherent.

This places the provider of the service in the upstream position. Each client is downstream, and typically some of them will be conformist and some will build anticorruption layers. A context with an open host service might have any sort of relationship to contexts other than its clients.

Published Language

The translation between the models of two bounded contexts requires a common language.

Direct translation to and from the existing domain models may not be a good solution. Those models may be overly complex or poorly factored. They are probably undocumented. If one is used as a data interchange language, it essentially becomes frozen and cannot respond to new development needs.

Therefore:
Use a well-documented shared language that can express the necessary domain information as a common medium of communication, translating as necessary into and out of that language.

Many industries establish published languages in the form of data interchange standards. Project teams also develop their own for use within their organization.

Published language is often combined with open-host service.

Separate Ways

We must be ruthless when it comes to defining requirements. If two sets of functionality have no significant relationship, they can be completely cut loose from each other.

Photo: US National Oceanic and Atmospheric Administration

Integration is always expensive, and sometimes the benefit is small.

Therefore:
Declare a bounded context to have no connection to the others at all, allowing developers to find simple, specialized solutions within this small scope.

Big Ball of Mud

Photo: Alicia Nijdam

As we survey existing software systems, trying to understand how distinct models are being applied within defined boundaries, we find parts of systems, often large ones, where models are mixed and boundaries are inconsistent.

It is easy to get bogged down in an attempt to describe the context boundaries of models in systems where there simply are no boundaries.

Well-defined context boundaries only emerge as a result of intellectual choices and social forces (even though the people creating the systems may not always have been consciously aware of these causes at the time). When these factors are absent, or disappear, multiple conceptual systems and mix together, making definitions and rules ambiguous or contradictory. The systems are made to work by contingent logic as features are added. Dependencies crisscross the software. Cause and effect become more and more difficult to trace. Eventually the software congeals into a big ball of mud.

The big ball of mud is actually quite practical for some situations (as described in the original article by Foote and Yoder), but it almost completely prevents the subtlety and precision needed for useful models.

Therefore:
Draw a boundary around the entire mess and designate it a big ball of mud. Do not try to apply sophisticated modeling within this context. Be alert to the tendency for such systems to sprawl into other contexts.

(see http://www.laputan.org/mud/mud.html. Brian Foote and Joseph Yoder)

V
Distillation for Strategic Design

$$\nabla \cdot \mathbf{D} = \rho \qquad \nabla \times \mathbf{H} = \mathbf{J} + \frac{\partial \mathbf{D}}{\partial t}$$

$$\nabla \cdot \mathbf{B} = 0 \qquad \nabla \times \mathbf{E} = -\frac{\partial \mathbf{B}}{\partial t}$$

—James Clerk Maxwell, A Treatise on Electricity and Magnetism, 1873

These four equations, along with the definitions of their terms and the body of mathematics they rest on, express the entirety of classical nineteenth-century electromagnetism.

How do you focus on your central problem and keep from drowning in a sea of side issues?

Distillation is the process of separating the components of a mixture to extract the essence in a form that makes it more valuable and useful. A model is a distillation of knowledge. With every refactoring to deeper insight, we abstract some crucial aspect of domain knowledge and priorities. Now, stepping back for a strategic view, this chapter looks at ways to distinguish broad swaths of the model and distill the domain model as a whole.

Core Domain

In a large system, there are so many contributing components, all complicated and all absolutely necessary to success, that the essence of the domain model, the real business asset, can be obscured and neglected.

It is harsh reality that not all parts of the design are going to be equally refined. Priorities must be set. To make the domain model an asset, the critical core of that model has to be sleek and fully leveraged to create application functionality. But scarce, highly skilled developers tend to gravitate to technical infrastructure or neatly definable domain problems that can be understood without specialized domain knowledge.

Therefore:
Boil the model down. Define a core domain and provide a means of easily distinguishing it from the mass of supporting model and code. Bring the most valuable and specialized concepts into sharp relief. Make the core small.

Apply top talent to the core domain, and recruit accordingly. Spend the effort in the core to find a deep model and develop a supple design—sufficient to fulfill the vision of the system.

Justify investment in any other part by how it supports the distilled core.

Generic Subdomains

Some parts of the model add complexity without capturing or communicating specialized knowledge. Anything extraneous makes the core domain harder to discern and understand. The model clogs up with general principles everyone knows or details that belong to specialties which are not your primary focus but play a supporting role. Yet, however generic, these other elements are essential to the functioning of the system and the full expression of the model.

Therefore:

Identify cohesive subdomains that are not the motivation for your project. Factor out generic models of these subdomains and place them in separate modules. Leave no trace of your specialties in them.

Once they have been separated, give their continuing development lower priority than the core domain, and avoid assigning your core developers to the tasks (because they will gain little domain knowledge from them). Also consider off-the-shelf solutions or published models for these generic subdomains.

Domain Vision Statement

At the beginning of a project, the model usually doesn't even exist, yet the need to focus its development is already there. In later stages of development, there is a need for an explanation of the value of the system that does not require an in-depth study of the model. Also, the critical aspects of the domain model may span multiple bounded contexts, but by definition these distinct models can't be structured to show their common focus.

Therefore:

Write a short description (about one page) of the core domain and the value it will bring, the "value proposition." Ignore those aspects that do not distinguish this domain model from others. Show how the domain model serves and balances diverse interests. Keep it narrow. Write this statement early and revise it as you gain new insight.

Highlighted Core

A domain vision statement identifies the core domain in broad terms, but it leaves the identification of the specific core model elements up to the vagaries of individual interpretation. Unless there is an exceptionally high level of communication on the team, the vision statement alone will have little impact.

Even though team members may know broadly what constitutes the core domain, different people won't pick out quite the same elements, and even the same person won't be consistent from one day to the next. The mental labor of constantly filtering the model to identify the key parts absorbs concentration better spent on design thinking, and it requires comprehensive knowledge of the model. The core domain must be made easier to see.

Significant structural changes to the code are the ideal way of identifying the core domain, but they are not always practical in the short term. In fact, such major code changes are difficult to undertake without the very view the team is lacking.

Therefore (as one form of highlighted core):
Write a very brief document (three to seven sparse pages) that describes the core domain and the primary interactions among core elements.

and/or (as another form of highlighted core):

Flag the elements of the core domain within the primary repository of the model, without particularly trying to elucidate its role. Make it effortless for a developer to know what is in or out of the core.

If the distillation document outlines the essentials of the core domain, then it serves as a practical indicator of the significance of a model change. When a model or code change affects the distillation document, it requires consultation with other team members. When the change is made, it requires immediate notification of all team members, and the dissemination of a new version of the document. Changes outside the core or to details not included in the distillation document can be integrated without consultation or notification and will be encountered by other members in the course of their work. Then the developers have the full autonomy that most Agile processes suggest.

Although the vision statement and highlighted core inform and guide, they do not actually modify the model or the code itself. Partitioning generic subdomains physically removes some distracting elements. Next we'll look at other ways to structurally change the model and the design itself to make the core domain more visible and manageable. . . .

Cohesive Mechanisms

Computations sometimes reach a level of complexity that begins to bloat the design. The conceptual "what" is swamped by the mechanistic "how." A large number of methods that provide algorithms for resolving the problem obscure the methods that express the problem.

Therefore:

Partition a conceptually cohesive mechanism into a separate lightweight framework. Particularly watch for formalisms or well-documented categories of algorithms. Expose the capabilities of the framework with an intention-revealing interface. Now the other elements of the domain can focus on expressing the problem ("what"), delegating the intricacies of the solution ("how") to the framework.

Factoring out generic subdomains reduces clutter, and cohesive mechanisms serve to encapsulate complex operations. This leaves behind a more focused model, with fewer distractions that add no particular value to the way users conduct their activities. But you are unlikely ever to find good homes for everything in the domain model that is not core. The segregated core takes a direct approach to structurally marking off the core domain. . . .

Segregated Core

Elements in the model may partially serve the core domain and partially play supporting roles. Core elements may be tightly coupled to generic ones. The conceptual cohesion of the core may not be strong or visible. All this clutter and entanglement chokes the core. Designers can't clearly see the most important relationships, leading to a weak design.

Therefore:

Refactor the model to separate the core concepts from supporting players (including ill-defined ones) and strengthen the cohesion of the core while reducing its coupling to other code. Factor all generic or supporting elements into other objects and place them into other packages, even if this means refactoring the model in ways that separate highly coupled elements.

Abstract Core

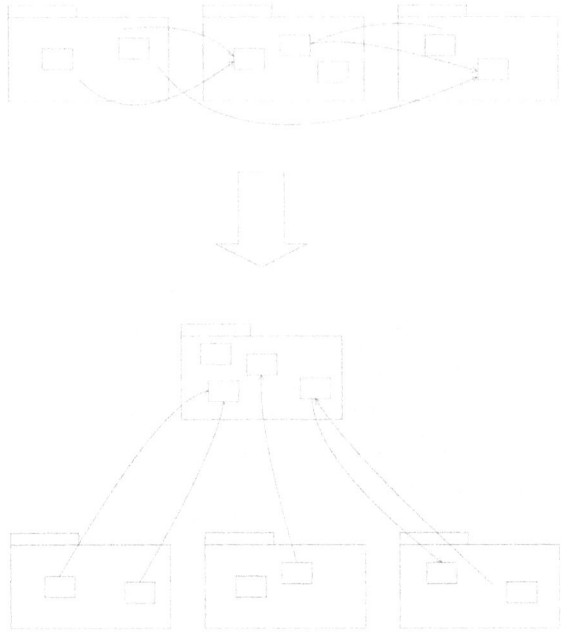

Even the core domain model usually has so much detail that communicating the big picture can be difficult.

When there is a lot of interaction between subdomains in separate modules, either many references will have to be created between modules, which defeats much of the value of the partitioning, or the interaction will have to be made indirect, which makes the model obscure.

Therefore:
Identify the most fundamental differentiating concepts in the model and factor them into distinct classes, abstract classes, or interfaces. Design this abstract model so that it

expresses most of the interaction between significant components. Place this abstract overall model in its own module, while the specialized, detailed implementation classes are left in their own modules defined by subdomain.

VI
Large-scale Structure for Strategic Design

Photo: Paul Margolies, AIDS Quilt

In a large system without any overarching principle that allows elements to be interpreted in terms of their role in patterns that span the whole design, developers cannot see the forest for the trees. We need to be able to understand the role of an individual part in the whole without delving into the details of the whole.

A "large-scale structure" is a language that lets you discuss and understand the system in broad strokes. A set of high-level concepts or rules, or both, establishes a pattern of design for an entire system. This organizing principle can guide design as well as aid understanding. It helps coordinate independent work because there is a shared concept of the big picture: how the roles of various parts shape the whole.

Therefore:
Devise a pattern of rules or roles and relationships that will span the entire system and that allows some understanding of each part's place in the whole—even without detailed knowledge of the part's responsibility.

Evolving Order

Design free-for-alls produce systems no one can make sense of as a whole, and they are very difficult to maintain. But architectures can straitjacket a project with up-front design assumptions and take too much power away from the developers/designers of particular parts of the application. Soon, developers will dumb down the application to fit the structure, or they will subvert it and have no structure at all, bringing back the problems of uncoordinated development.

Therefore:
Let this conceptual large-scale structure evolve with the application, possibly changing to a completely different type of structure along the way. Don't over constrain the detailed design and model decisions that must be made with detailed knowledge.

Large-scale structure should be applied when a structure can be found that greatly clarifies the system without forcing unnatural constraints on model development. Because an ill-fitting structure is worse than none, it is best not to shoot for comprehensiveness, but rather to find a minimal set that solves the problems that have emerged. Less is more.

What follows is a set of four particular patterns of large-scale structure that emerge on some projects and are representative of this kind of pattern.

System Metaphor

Metaphorical thinking is pervasive in software development, especially with models. But the Extreme Programming practice of "metaphor" has come to mean a particular way of using a metaphor to bring order to the development of a whole system.

Software designs tend to be very abstract and hard to grasp. Developers and users alike need tangible ways to understand the system and share a view of the system as a whole.

Therefore:
When a concrete analogy to the system emerges that captures the imagination of team members and seems to lead thinking in a useful direction, adopt it as a large-scale structure. Organize the design around this metaphor and absorb it into the ubiquitous language. The system metaphor should both facilitate communication about the system and guide development of it. This increases consistency in different parts of the system, potentially even across different bounded contexts. But because all metaphors are inexact, continually reexamine the metaphor for overextension or inaptness, and be ready to drop it if it gets in the way.

Responsibility Layers

In object-oriented design, individual objects are assigned narrow sets of related responsibilities. Responsibility-driven design also applies to larger scales.

When each individual object has handcrafted responsibilities, there are no guidelines, no uniformity, and no ability to handle large swaths of the domain together. To give coherence to a large model, it is useful to impose some structure on the assignment of those responsibilities.

Therefore:

Look at the conceptual dependencies in your model and the varying rates and sources of change of different parts of your domain. If you identify natural strata in the domain, cast them as broad abstract responsibilities. These responsibilities should tell a story of the high-level purpose and design of your system. Refactor the model so that the responsibilities of each domain object, aggregate, and module fit neatly within the responsibility of one layer.

Knowledge Level

A group of objects that describe how another group of objects should behave.

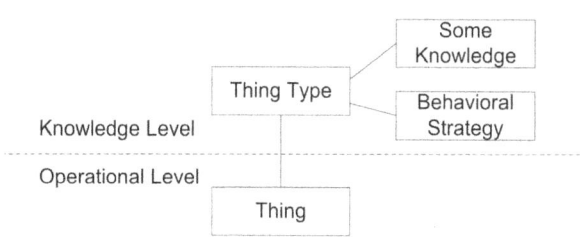

In an application in which the roles and relationships between entities vary in different situations, complexity can explode. Neither fully general models nor highly customized ones serve the users' needs. Objects end up with references to other types to cover a variety of cases, or with attributes that are used in different ways in different situations. Classes that have the same data and behavior may multiply just to accommodate different assembly rules.

Therefore:

Create a distinct set of objects that can be used to describe and constrain the structure and behavior of the basic model. Keep these concerns separate as two "levels," one very concrete, the other reflecting rules and knowledge that a user or super-user is able to customize.

(see Fowler, M. 1997. Analysis Patterns: Reusable Object Models, *Addison-Wesley.)*

Pluggable Component Framework

Opportunities arise in a very mature model that is deep and distilled. A pluggable component framework usually only comes into play after a few applications have already been implemented in the same domain.

When a variety of applications have to interoperate, all based on the same abstractions but designed independently, translations between multiple bounded contexts limit integration. A shared kernel is not feasible for teams that do not work closely together. Duplication and fragmentation raise costs of development and installation, and interoperability becomes very difficult.

Therefore:

Distill an abstract core of interfaces and interactions and create a framework that allows diverse implementations of those interfaces to be freely substituted. Likewise, allow any application to use those components, so long as it operates strictly through the interfaces of the abstract core.

Photo Credits

Rowing Eight, Christopher Schmidt (Creative Commons Attribution 2.0)

Fingerprints, Wanted Poster, US Department of Justice

Grapes, Martine Jousset, used with permission

Out at Home Plate, 1925, Library of Congress Prints & Photographs

Three-Legged Race, 1909, Marin County Free Library

Great Wall of China, U.S. National Oceanic and Atmospheric Administration

Sculler, Curran Kelleher, (Creative Commons Attribution 2.0)

AIDS Quilt, Photographer Paul Margolies. © 2003 NAMES Project Foundation, Atlanta, Georgia, www.aidsquilt.org, used with permission

Other Credits

Most pattern summaries are excerpted from the book *Domain-Driven Design: Tackling Complexity in the Heart of Software*, by Eric Evans, Addison-Wesley 2004.

DDD training for teams and individuals from Domain Language

ADVERTISEMENT

Interactive training classes with instructors personally coached by Eric Evans, the author of the original DDD book.

- Public open enrollment classes
- Private, on-site classes

Check domainlanguage.com for course offerings, schedules and pricing of public classes.

Video-based, self-paced training.

- The essential topics of DDD
- Lectures and explanations by Eric Evans
- Team dynamics brought to life in staged reenactments

Find out more at domainlanguage.com/elearn

domain **language**

Lightning Source UK Ltd.
Milton Keynes UK
UKHW040727311218
334816UK00010B/204/P